Sea Turtles

Fun Facts & Amazing Pictures

Learn About Sea Turtles

Terry Mason

Sea Turtles introduction

Sea turtles, also known as marine turtles, are aquatic reptiles that can be found in oceans all over the world, except in the Arctic. These animals are endangered because their population is slowly getting smaller. Even though they are marine animals, sea turtles still need to go on land, namely beaches or dunes, to breathe air and to make nests for their eggs. Let us get to know more about these beautiful animals of the sea.

Turtle-cleaning-Station

Body Parts of Sea Turtles

The sea turtles have evolved with the type of body that they have so that they can easily adapt to their environment. They may be slow to crawl on land but they are fast swimmers. Unlike other animals, they have both interior and exterior skeletons.

Their outer skeleton, which is made of the same materials as their bones, is in the form of a shell. The upper shell is called a carapace and the lower shell is called a plastron. The shell serves as their protection from predators and from the environment on land or in water. Their inner skeleton helps them maintain their shape. It is also what connects their shell with the muscles in their body.

To be able to swim well in water and crawl on land, they have very large flippers which are also very sensitive to touch. Their eyes are also special as each has eyelids. When you hear people say that sea turtles cry, this is actually how they are able to flush out the salt of what they eat.

Sea Turtles' Habitat

Sea turtles live in different shallow seas all over the world. They live in seaweed beds so that they can feed on the seaweeds. They prefer to stay in tropical waters and will migrate to warmer oceans whenever the water gets colder. Male turtles, after taking to the water for the first time, will not go back to shore again. Only females come ashore to build their nest and lay their eggs.

Sea-turtle-on-coral-reef

Migration

Sea turtles are migratory animals. They transfer from one place to another even over long distances for the purpose of feeding and nesting. When baby sea turtles hatch from their underground nest, they migrate from the land to the sea. This is why female sea turtles make their nest on the shoreline to make it easier for their babies to travel to the water.

The feeding and nesting sites of sea turtles are often separated by large distances, giving these creatures the need to travel hundreds, sometimes even thousands of miles. Each of the sea turtle families has their different migration patterns. And it is also an amazing thing to know that they are able to return to the very same feeding or breeding area just by relying on their instincts!

School Of Sea Turtles Migration

Sea Turtles' Senses

The sea turtles also have the same basic senses that we humans have: they can see, hear, smell, taste and feel too. They are colorblind but their eyesight is sharper underwater than it is on the surface. They hear vibrations and low-frequency sounds. Their flippers and shell are sensitive to touch and their sense of smell is very sharp underwater, and this allows them to hunt for food much more easily.

Turtle Talk

How Sea Turtles Breathe

For them to be able to adapt living in water or on land, their respiratory system has also been given special characteristics. The sea turtles are air-breathers and whenever the need arises; their lungs can be easily filled with air. They can stay underwater for long hours and they can quickly suck air into their lungs once they resurface.

Hawksbill-Sea-Turtle

What They Eat

Sea turtles are considered omnivores because they feed on aquatic plants and animals. Each sea turtle family has their favorite meals. From fishes to small aquatic creatures, from algae to seaweeds of a different kind, sea turtles munch on a large selection of meals underwater. They feed on mollusks and crustaceans, too.

Hawksbill Sea Turtle Eating

The Sea Turtles' Movement

Sea turtles move to different places by crawling, swimming, and diving. When on land, they use their flippers to crawl through sand dunes. All sea turtles have crawled on the land at least once and that is soon after they have hatched from their eggs. They are also great swimmers and can swim at a speed of 1.5 to 3 kilometers per hour. They use their front limbs to paddle through water and their hind legs are what steers them.

Sea turtles are also great at diving and can go down to as deep as 1000 feet to look for food. Being cold-blooded creatures, their metabolism is quite slow, allowing them to stay underwater for hours. Their heart rate also slows down to help them consume less air during their dive. The black sea turtles are even known to bury themselves in mud or sand and remain dormant from November right through until March!

Baby-green-turtles-moving-toward the ocean

Their Social Behavior

After hatching, each baby sea turtle individually works its way into the water without assistance from their mother. They remain solitary until the time when they are ready to mate. Some families of sea turtles migrate to their mating and nesting grounds in one group. They are not generally social creatures but some of them are known to gather in groups.

Baby-Turtles

Nesting and Hatching Eggs

After mating, a pregnant female sea turtle migrates to her nesting place and builds a nest, where she can lay up to 200 eggs at once. Nests should be made on warm beaches so that the sea turtles will survive while still inside the eggs. Researchers found out that the sex of the baby will depend on the temperature. More males are produced from low temperatures and more females during warm temperatures.

Baby Turtle Eggs Hatching

The Clutch

Clutch refers to the group of eggs in a nest laid at once by a mother sea turtle. This word is also used to refer to the group of eggs laid by birds, amphibians, and other reptiles. The clutch can contain anywhere between 50 to 200 eggs, depending on the species of the sea turtle. The eggs look like Ping-Pong balls, soft-shelled, surrounded by mucus and the texture may range from leathery to papery.

Baby Turtle Eggs Hatching

The Baby Sea Turtles

After about 45 to 70 days, the baby sea turtles will break out of their eggs using their temporary egg tooth or carbuncle. They will then dig out of their nest and travel the length of the shore off to the water. Among the 200 eggs laid, only 5 will be able to survive to adulthood, this is the main reason why sea turtles lay so many eggs.

Loggerhead Turtle Baby

Green Sea Turtle

Green Sea Turtle – also known as the Black turtle or Pacific green turtle. It is large, flat and covered by a teardrop-shaped shell, which has different patterns of colors. It has a short and unhooked beak at the end of its head, a short neck, and paddle-like flippers. It can grow up to 5 feet long and can weigh up to 300 kilograms

Hawaiian Green Sea Turtle

Hawksbill Sea Turtle

Hawksbill Sea Turtle – Due to improper fishing practices by humans, this turtle is becoming critically endangered and threatened. This species is closely related to the Green sea turtles because their physical features are quite similar. The only main difference is the beak, wherein the hawksbill's beak is curved and sharp. While it spends some of its life in the open ocean, it spends more time in coral reefs and shallow waters.

Closeup Crop of Hawksbill Sea Turtle

Kemp's Ridley Sea Turtle

Kemp's Ridley Sea Turtle – this sea turtle is the rarest and smallest of all sea turtles and is also critically endangered. It grows up to 35 inches long and can weigh up to 45 pounds. It has an oval-shaped shell and is usually colored olive-gray. Its triangular head has a hooked beak and it feeds primarily on crabs.

Atlantic or Kemp Ridley Critically Endangered Sea Turtle

Loggerhead Sea Turtle

Loggerhead Sea Turtle – the Loggerhead can grow to a length of 35 inches and weigh up to 135 kilograms. Its color can range from yellow to brown, with the shell a typical reddish brown. An adult male loggerhead is distinguished through its thicker tail, while the female has a shorter belly.

Loggerhead Sea Turtle

Leatherback Sea Turtle

Leatherback Sea Turtle – also called the Lute turtle, this is the largest among all sea turtle species and is also the fourth largest among all modern reptiles. Another big difference of the leatherback is that it does not have the bony shell that the other turtle species possess. It has an oily skin covering instead, which is thick and leathery.

Leatherback Turtle On Beach

Olive Ridley Sea Turtle

Olive Ridley Sea Turtle – this medium-sized sea turtle is found in warm waters and can measure up to 70 centimeters and weigh up to 46 kilograms. Its heart-shaped shell is flattened and its head has a short snout. They group together to form huge groups of nests called arribadas.

Close up of Olive Ridley Sea Turtle Underwater

Fun Facts about Sea Turtles

1. Most sea turtles can travel up to 1300 miles a day

2. The sea turtles shells are as tough as a rock, so when they dive into deep parts of the ocean, they would never crack.

3. Leatherback sea turtles can dive up to 300 meters deep and they can stay underwater for up to around 5 hours.

4. To help them conserve their oxygen, sea turtles are able to slow down their heart rate, with each heart beat elapsing for about 10 minutes!

5. Turtles have been living around the Earth for about 200 million years.

6. Sea turtles cry because of their salt glands. These glands help them remove the salt from the sea water that they drink.

Comprehension Test

1. The leatherback sea turtle is also called a _____.

2. Which of the sea turtle species is the rarest?

3. Up to how many eggs can a mother sea turtle lay at one time?

4. A _____ is a group of eggs laid by a female sea turtle in a nest.

5. True or false. The sea turtles' upper shell is also called a plastron.

6. Are sea turtles reptiles or amphibians?

7. The group of nests made by sea turtles in one area are called _____.

8. Baby sea turtles that just came out of their shells are called _____.

9. The baby sea turtles use a temporary egg tooth to break out of their egg. What do you call this temporary tooth?

10. Which among the sea turtles does not have a bony shell?

Comprehension answer

1. Lute Turtle
2. Kemp's Ridley Sea Turtle
3. 200 eggs
4. Clutch
5. False
6. Reptiles
7. Arribadas
8. Hatchlings
9. Carbuncle
10. Leatherback Sea Turtles

Disclaimer

All rights reserved. No part of this e-book may be reproduced or transmitted in any form or by any means, electronic or mechanical, including photocopying, recording, or by any information storage and retrieval system, without the expressed written permission from the author and publishing company.

Made in the USA
Columbia, SC
08 December 2023

28027938R00015